WILLIAM H. DAVIES

7 ESSENTIAL METHODS

...to help Manage Technology in your Business

'Running a business isn't always easy. a balanced Technology Infrastructure can make a world of difference'.

7 Essential Methods to help Manage Technology in your Businesses

First published 2012 by Amazon

ISBN-13: 978-1475189094

ISBN-10: 1475189095

Contents

Introduction

Running a business of any size isn't easy. From finding customers, to presenting your goods or services in the right way, to the marketing of your entire presence, it's all time-consuming. And as you'll probably agree, your time is precious.

Add to the fundamentals mentioned above, accounting, administration, market research, keeping tabs on your competitors, and maintaining a reliable and robust technology infrastructure of any size, can sap your energy and enthusiasm.

You most likely started your business because you're an entrepreneur, or perhaps because you have much more to give than could ever be tapped by working for someone else. Or it could be other reasons, redundancy from an employed position, the purchase of a franchise, or maybe the foresight to have spotted a gap in the market for a product or service.

Whatever the reason, it's highly unlikely you started your business because you like spending time on paperwork, administration, and other peripheral (but essential) tasks.

The more time you spend on these, the less time you spend finding customers. The less time spent finding customers, the less time selling your product or service. The less time selling....of course means less money in the bank account.

With this in mind, this e-book has been written to help you get the most from your IT setup.

Technology is an amazing thing – from email, to video conferencing, to accounting, to keeping a solid database of all goings on, from customer details to sales analysis. It's all there, hinged on the technology you use in your business. The technology you use defines the way your business grows, but more importantly, the way you use that technology is crucial to the your businesses success.

Gone are the days where a business can survive without technology. It's essential to get everything in your IT setup right – from the type of computers you choose, to the backup strategy you decide on, to the marketing of your business online.

To help make your business life smoother and easier, here are seven great methods to do just that.

1. Ask yourself "What do I actually need from my technology?".

Asking yourself this, is an important first step in getting a complete end-to-end solution that can streamline your business and make making money, easier! That's what you're doing it for, right?

Examine your business needs;
If you're a florist, you would need your IT setup to be able to input customer orders, track the progress of them from the initial order over the phone or email, to the delivery of the bouquet.

You need a way to take payments over the phone and online, you need a way to track those payments so you can give the details to your accountant.

You need a PC or laptop so you can manage your online advertising. You also need to make sure that if there was a fire or theft at your premises, that you have a safe and reliable backup of your data.

You may even need a fall-back process, which is commonly referred to as a "Business Continuity Plan" in larger firms.

2. Match your requirements with your existing technology.

Now you've asked yourself that question, you should be able to put that list alongside what you currently have.

Using the same Florist example above, create a list in a spreadsheet with all the requirements going down column 'A'.

In the next column, put in what the ideal solution would be for that requirement, bearing in mind your budget and size of business.

In the next column, put in what you actually have in place. Be honest, there's no point in dressing it up to something it's not.

Now you have that in place, in the next column, put in an action point for yourself. That could be "Investigate ways to process repeat orders from existing clients", or "Contact my IT guy to find out about a PC that's quick enough to run a database and email at the same time".

In the final column, put a date next to the action point. Now you have a small plan in front of you that can help solidify and reinforce your technical set-up.

3. **Using the right sort of email**

This might seem an odd statement, but today, using different types of email can drastically change the way you work, the administration around communications, and your costs too.

Most businesses have a domain name, or sometimes two or three. Your ISP (Internet Service Provider) will have a facility for you to use Microsoft Outlook on your PC or laptop, to connect up and download/upload email. This is a popular way of working your businesses email.

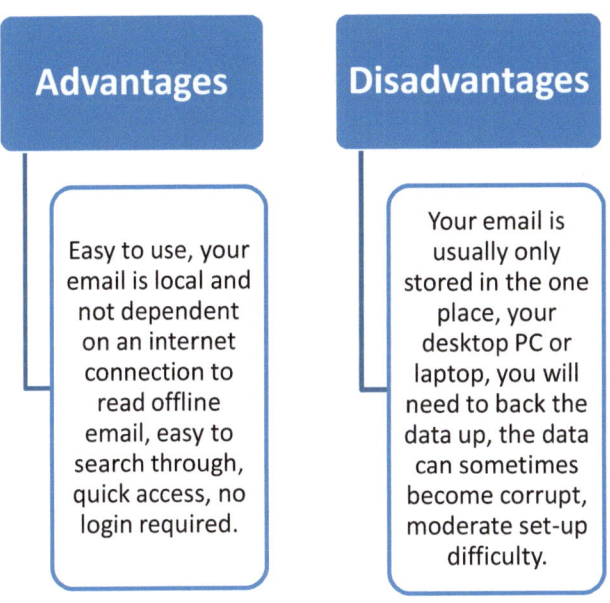

Advantages

Easy to use, your email is local and not dependent on an internet connection to read offline email, easy to search through, quick access, no login required.

Disadvantages

Your email is usually only stored in the one place, your desktop PC or laptop, you will need to back the data up, the data can sometimes become corrupt, moderate set-up difficulty.

Another way is the very simple online accounts – G-Mail, Hotmail, and Yahoo email are some of the most common.

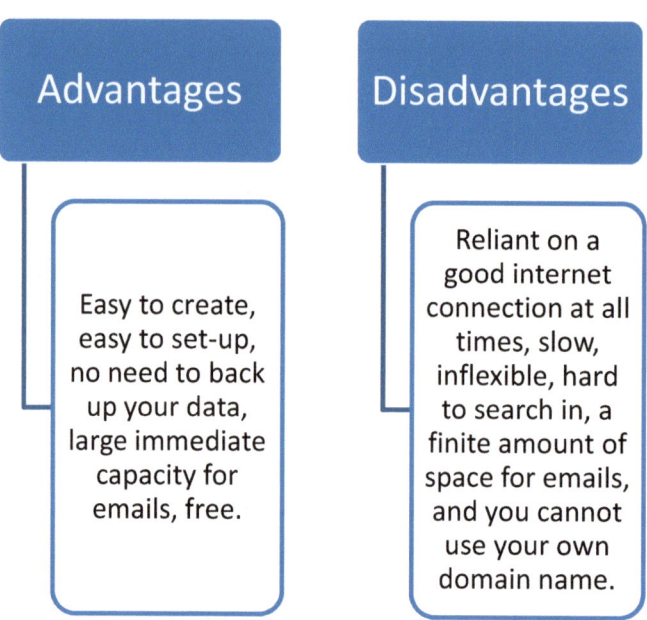

Advantages	Disadvantages
Easy to create, easy to set-up, no need to back up your data, large immediate capacity for emails, free.	Reliant on a good internet connection at all times, slow, inflexible, hard to search in, a finite amount of space for emails, and you cannot use your own domain name.

The final way we'll talk about, is to have fully-hosted services. These are a mix of the two methods above, and involve all email services for your domain name being 'pointed' to a hosted email provider. You then are able to see your email on a mixture of devices, from your PC, to your iPad, your HP Touchpad, and your Android phone. Usually feature-rich, this is now the best way to manage your business email.

Advantages

Fast, efficient, flexible, uses your domain name, no backups ever required, configurable amount of storage, all the features of Outlook with the benefits of online email.

Disadvantages

A monthly fee is incurred, you have to have all your email addresses for that domain on the service.

4. Secure your mobile devices

Every now and again, if you read the Tech press, you will read about a firm who 'lost a laptop' or USB stick on a train, or left it on a café, for someone to then view it and find all sorts of data that really shouldn't have gone out of the business premises.

There are numerous reasons why it did though, the most common is that sometimes we like to take our work home, so we get to see the kids in the evening rather than sat in a lonely office or workshop. The other common reason is of course, people who are on the road a lot for their job.

When a laptop or USB device (or anything that can hold client or customer data) get's lost and is reported to the authorities by the finder, the company can be fined thousands of pounds by the UK Government, for failure to adhere to the Data Protection act.

At the very least, if you have customer or client data that is carried out of the office as a one-off or regularly, you should adopt an encryption program for each device, and ensure it is used.

The last company in the press to have failed to have done this was fined over £120,000.

Their annual *turnover* was only £230,000. So that must have hurt, *a lot*.

5. Backup your data

If you're a business that uses a database, or file system to keep track of client goings-on, transactions, billing information, order tracking, lead follow-up lists, invoices and quotes, that is your companies blood. Without this data, the business becomes an empty host.

Imagine for a minute that the worst happened. During one evening, a room above your office or workshop floods. Your three PCs, one server, and printer/scanner are in the room below, and they are slowly drenched by the water coming through the ceiling and the subsequent collapse of the ceiling.

You come into work in the morning to find a huge mess. But that's not the biggest problem you have – today you have to get out an order to one of your biggest clients, for.....now what was it......120 of one product, 300 of another....or was it the other way around?

With no backup of your data, you're now in a very hard place.

Not only can you not get the order out to your client on the day without phoning them and looking a little amateur, but you also have lost all your costings, and the quote you sent them in the first place.

Backup all your data, from files, to databases, to emails.

6. Ensure you have a responsive and reliable IT Support company behind you.

A common misconception by many businesses is that all IT people are the same, they all know the same stuff, after all, it's just computers, right?

That misconception couldn't be further from the truth. No two IT Companies are the same. IT can be split into hundreds of different sectors, and then thousands of splinter-sectors after that.

The IT Support one company offers will never be the same as the next company.

As a business looking to grow and make more money, you know that IT is one of the cornerstones to making that happen. To facilitate your growth and success, you need to choose the right kind of IT Support Company.

You should ask;

    a) What areas do you cover?
    b) What are your specific areas of expertise?
    c) How have you helped businesses like mine before?
    d) What are the backgrounds of your staff?

Alongside that, you should also ask for the following, as a bare minimum from any decent IT Support company;

i)   Do you have GUARANTEED response times to support calls?

ii)   Do you have the experience to help me grow my business through IT?

iii)   Do you have a strong customer-focused work ethic?

You need your IT Support company to have an extremely strong customer-focus, you also need to have a guaranteed response time for an engineer to respond. There's no point in logging a call and then waiting half a day for someone to get around to looking at the issue.

Your time is money, and your money is why you're in business. A good IT Support company will effectively help you look after your money.

Another thing to be wary of are companies that claim to 'do it all' with two or three people. You can relate this to going to your local GP.

Now he or she will be a great doctor, I'm sure. But would you want him or her to perform an eye operation on you? Or perform liver-analysis? Of course not, because whilst the GP will *know* about all the above, he will have extremely limited information and experience on the subject, and will refer you to a specialist.

The same works for IT Support companies – if they said they can do it all, ask *how* they can do it all? Ask them how they achieve this? Only companies with strong structure and support behind them themselves, will be able to offer a complete end-to-end solution. The rest will most likely be 'hobbyists' in some areas.

7. Balancing speed with speed

Many companies, when needing a new PC or laptop, or server, will rush out and ask for the best and fastest device available. They then have it installed, and wonder why it's no quicker than the five year old device they now have as a doorstop.

It's important to know your infrastructure and setup. If you have fast PC's but a slow network, then you should address the network first. If you have a super-fast network but a slow server, address the server first. Always eliminate the slowest part of the path from A to B.

This also holds true for smaller devices. If you backup some data for example, to an external USB Hard disk, and you find it slow – before you rush out to buy a new and faster one, check if your PC or laptop can actually handle the faster speeds. There are three different USB transfer speeds, and whilst they're all backwards compatible, if your laptop is USBv1.0 ,and your new external disk is v3.0…….guess which speed it's going to run at!

Similarly, is your broadband connection. I have known companies to spend a fortune on internal networking, to find their end-to-end process is still no quicker. I have been called in to find out why the other company failed, and after a little investigation, found the issue to be the external broadband. A phrase to remember is *"The pack is only as quick as its slowest animal"*. And the same goes for end-to-end IT Processes.

For more booklets or white papers on Technical subjects, please contact info@interwebi.com or periodically check out Amazon!

www.ingramcontent.com/pod-product-compliance
Lightning Source LLC
Chambersburg PA
CBHW041121180526
45172CB00001B/361